Shawn,
Never o'
Creatin...

THE MASTER WITHIN

Crayning News: Shown ink

Create Your Masterpiece

TITUS BARTOLOTTA
WITH CHRISTINA BARTOLOTTA

outskirts
press

The Master Within
All Rights Reserved.
Copyright © 2019 Titus Bartolotta
v1.0

The opinions expressed in this manuscript are solely the opinions of the author and do not represent the opinions or thoughts of the publisher. The author has represented and warranted full ownership and/or legal right to publish all the materials in this book.

This book may not be reproduced, transmitted, or stored in whole or in part by any means, including graphic, electronic, or mechanical without the express written consent of the publisher except in the case of brief quotations embodied in critical articles and reviews.

Outskirts Press, Inc.
http://www.outskirtspress.com

ISBN: 978-1-9772-0460-8

Cover Photo © 2019 Nelson Leonard Bynum. All rights reserved - used with permission.

Outskirts Press and the "OP" logo are trademarks belonging to Outskirts Press, Inc.

PRINTED IN THE UNITED STATES OF AMERICA

THE ARTS

Foreword i
Intro v
Preparation 1
    Preparation *11*
Sculpting: Sales 15
    Carve Out Your Path *21*
Painting: Leadership 27
    Apply the Brushstrokes *35*
Comedy: Communication 39
    Perfect Practice *46*
Acting: Influence 53
    Control Your Narrative *58*

Photography: Mindset 65
   Keep Your Vision in Focus *72*
Sports: Teamwork 79
   Maintain the Endurance to Win *88*
Execution 95
Thank you 111

Foreword

Several years ago, I visited Florence, Italy and was simply awestruck by the paintings and sculptures from the great masters who created them centuries ago. Gazing up at the statue of David left me breathless, and I was reminded of what the renowned Michelangelo said when asked about his majestic art, "I saw the Angel in the marble and carved until I set him free."

Later, reading about Michelangelo, as well as many of the other Renaissance painters and sculptors, I was intrigued by the process that they used to grow their skill. They apprenticed, learning and honing their craft, until they were deemed capable of execution at an acceptable level, by the master from which they studied. This process could last up to ten years.

Early in my career, the words of a football coach, Ray Parlier, from Furman University left an indelible mark in my mind when he said, "If you ever see a turtle sitting on a fence post, you know he had help getting there." Few of us will ever achieve anything worthwhile in our lives without people who help to push us past limitations we might otherwise impose upon ourselves. They are coaches, mentors, advisors and friends who selflessly make an intentional effort for us to discover the masterpiece that lay dormant inside.

As a past president of the United States Junior Chamber of Commerce (Jaycees), a leadership training organization for young professionals 21 to 39 years of age, I have always believed in the power of young people. The strength of our nation lies in the hands of youth and action; and that is very evident in a young man I met less than a decade ago in Lake Norman – Titus Bartolotta.

In just a short time, Titus has emerged as a business and community leader. That is even more remarkable when one considers his early childhood. Titus is very open with the fact that neither he, nor his wife

Christina, came from a story book beginning. Titus endured poverty at many levels, often finding himself in an environment that was financially unstable. The experiences they had growing up, would come to make lasting impressions on them both, and they made a promise to each other. They promised that they would do everything they possibly could to bring hope and happiness to children and families who need a helping hand. Titus and Christina are keeping that promise, and their organization, The Lotta Foundation, along with the volunteers and contributors who make their work possible, are doing "A Lotta Good!"

In the last couple of years, Titus has created Business Leaders Unleashed (BLU) which is transforming how business leaders connect and build mutually beneficial relationships, while inspiring each other to be their personal best.

"*The Master Within*" by Titus Bartolotta is not just another leadership book, but rather a personal journey for the reader in which he peels away the layers of marble exposing that masterpiece which exists in all of us. Filled with personal development and leadership lessons, Titus provides insight with the mind of an emerging entrepreneur and the heart of a servant leader.

Like Titus, I believe God gave each and every one of us certain unique skills and abilities to change the face of our community. That is our gift from God. How we choose to use those special talents is our gift back to God.

Now open your eyes, free your mind, and prepare your heart to discover the master within you.

W.E. "Bill" Russell, CCE, IOM
President & CEO
Lake Norman Chamber of Commerce

Intro

I've seen a lot of bad in my life, and in the world. An amount which, while is not as much as some, it is still more than many people could fathom. The decision, as I saw it, was mine to make. I believed that I had an opportunity to experience, and see much more good, rather than simply be stuck with all of the bad in my world. I knew that I could experience this good as often as I desired. So much so, that it would become so big that the negatives would shift from the essence of my reality, and move to becoming so small that they would be difficult to see. I could do this for as long as I wanted, just so long as I ensured that the good would always come from me. Once I was the good that I longed for, I became what I hoped the world would be; and, then, I grew to be the light that

I so desperately needed to see. Mastering this process allowed me to, in those dark moments, look within me. Succumbing to the dark can't happen when light is present. This is important for me to share, because if I did it, you can too. Now, let's talk about how you are going to create your masterpiece so that you can share it with the world.

Preparation

What if... What if I told you that you could create the masterpiece that has been lying dormant inside?

The Oxford Dictionary defines masterpiece as;

"A work of outstanding artistry or skill."

Merriam-Webster provides the following definitions for masterpiece;

> " 1 : a work done with extraordinary skill; especially : a supreme intellectual or artistic achievement 2 : a piece of work presented to a medieval guild as evidence of qualification for the rank of master."

The Master Within

As we consider the masters who have shared their works with the world, we can note that they have similar characteristics. These traits carry across all types of works, so regardless of whether they are sculpting, painting, or cooking, they each have similar characteristics that lead to their ability to continue creating masterpieces. When we really look into them, we may notice, and begin to list, things like discipline, passion, high standards, motivation, perseverance, and so on. Another big factor in one's ability to create a masterpiece, and share that masterpiece with the world, is that person's ability to control their mindset.

What if you mastered the characteristics necessary to make a masterpiece too? Two simple words could completely change your life. What if… Keep in mind, however, that you have a tremendous amount of power over your own success. This means that the words that enter your world, or even come out of your mouth, only really have the power that you assign them. "WHAT IF" could become a way of life, if you wanted it to. What if you decided today, right now, that you would give these words the power they deserve? What if you allowed yourself to see past the letters and find the heart and soul of the words? Could something life changing happen? What if you actually created your masterpiece? Do you see it? Can

Preparation

you feel it? That blend of the power you hold over your own life, wrapped inside the sound of your own breath, coupled with the grace of a loving God. The combination creates such a charge that it generates a heartbeat that can be found deep within the words, your words; and gives them, not only greater depth, not only deeper meaning, but… life.

With this combination, you can ignite a fire that fuels your dreams, passions, and that ultimately allows for the discovery of the opportunities that exist for your future. You can bring light into dark places. Dark places that are uncharted territories, simply because they provide no light. Places that are filled with untapped opportunity, that you are currently unable to see. You can take advantage of those opportunities, because with your light, the places aren't so dark anymore. With your light, you can experience clarity that comes when you have the ability to see, so there are no missteps when traveling across the bridge. When you choose to shine your light, the darkness can no longer consume your space.

Thinking about this in a way which communicates mindset to be the thing that gives will its power, means the intestinal fortitude that it takes to move when you would rather stand still is within your control.

Moreover, it is fueled and readily accessible, so long as your mindset is one that gives strength to growth, passion, reflection, perseverance and discipline. Let's decide to give these words the power they deserve, and thereby ignite something truly special, and really meaningful. If you started preparing yourself with a 'what if' mentality, instead of allowing a 'no way to do it' mindset, do you now see what could happen? Is it possible that you could accomplish something you might have otherwise viewed as impossible or improbable? The answer is, of course, yes.

The thing that stands in the way of our breakthrough and vision is, often times, our inaction. We lack the belief that we are able to do amazing things, and therefore, often times, simply fail to take action. This inaction in and of itself stimulates something amazing. It is amazing that something so well designed and filled with such ability and power by a loving God could stagnate, be halted, and held back from its own victory, and privilege. Clearly for us to operate in greatness it requires action. When we come to the awareness that inaction is, in itself, an action; we can then hold on to the greater awareness that lies just beneath the surface. It is not the world we live in, those walking alongside us, or even evil that holds enough power to stop our ability to accomplish great

Preparation

things. It is us. For your life, this means, it is you. You can determine your outcome. You can control your destiny. You can create your masterpiece.

My earliest memory was that of a small boy staring into a tall mirror. I remember seeing only myself, at first. As I stood there looking at myself, slowly, I began to notice the things around me. I looked past myself and saw the table and chairs behind me. I was completely fascinated by the minute details of the room, as I looked up, down, and around myself in that mirror. It was in that moment that I found myself aware of things. When I say that, I mean, that I was really aware of my surroundings, and began to see them with a detail that I had not been privy to before. I turned and looked at the room with my bare eye, yet somehow when I looked directly at those things with those same eyes, it just didn't have the same impact. My mind began then to pull apart this strange new concept, and I thought to myself; "When I am in the picture, the things around me seem to be enhanced. Or, at least, my awareness and attention to detail grows." Then I realized, that as a result of the simple act of looking into that mirror, I hadn't simply entered the picture. My place had not changed, but somehow, my perception did. How could this be? You see, my perception was directly impacted by my awareness, and seeing myself in that mirror heightened that awareness. It presented the opportunity for a new angle, and in that view, I was able to see myself in my place. Prior to this moment, when I walked into a room, it was only the room around me that I could see. That mirror allowed me to see the reality of me being in the room, and there was a connection to the room that naturally followed as a result.

This moment of understanding was something I decided that I would keep with me always. Later in life, as I found experience that came through the years to add to this understanding, I established that when I truly see myself, things become clear, and I am able to understand them at a higher level. I continued to hold, nurture and grow this truth. That truth later grew into a new realization for me. Suddenly, just as simply as I know that I need to breathe in order to live, I knew that I would need to see myself in a moment, if I wanted to have the clarity necessary to see all the details of that situation. That clarity is a necessary part of the outcome, and it can be seen as a part of the preparation needed to make decisions that impact the situations.

It would be in visualizing my moment that I would be able to thrive in that moment. Today I believe that

Preparation

real vision only comes when you place yourself in the scene. We as humans are naturally drawn to being connected, involved, and to adding value. This is such a good thing. It is this need that gives us the ability to spark a flame into our own future and create real vision for our desires.

In those childhood years, I fell in love with the game of chess. My grandfather taught me how to play, over the course of several weeks. He patiently took the time to show me exactly how each piece on the board moved, explain what each piece's power was, and demonstrate the ability and purpose of those pieces. He showed me that every one of those wooden figures was really a tool, that if used correctly, would allow me to achieve my goal of winning. So, I knew the capability of the pieces. I understood their potential in a dynamic way. Once I demonstrated a clear comprehension for both the rules of the game and the way to play it, my grandfather began to play chess with me. He had simply one more rule. He would only play the game with me once every day. This meant that win or lose, the outcome was accepted until our next match, twenty-four hours later. Well, I lost… a lot. I absolutely hated losing. Even worse than the loss, for me, was the lack of redemption. I had to sit with my loss, over and over; time and again, for the full twenty-four hours.

The Master Within

My grandfather never let me win, nor did he waiver on his twenty-four-hour commitment. It got the point that it seemed no matter how many times I played, no matter how many different strategies I took, I just simply could not win. Almost as though defeat was my destiny. I associated this game with thinking, and intellect. I made a connection between being good at chess and being smart. This correlation was logical to me at the time. My grandfather was the smartest person I knew, and he happened to be great at the game. Additionally, our society backed my theory. I understood that when you were the best first baseman in the major leagues they called you an "All Star" but when you were the best in chess, they called you a "Chess Master". As you might imagine, as my losses became inevitable to me, so too did my ability to be smart become an impossibility.

In time, I began to try to avoid the game. Each time, my grandfather recognized that, and gently continued to push me to play. Over time, I found that I began to know what my grandfather was going to do. I discovered patterns in his play. I thought for sure that with my willingness to continue to play, an understanding of the rules, the comprehension of the ability for each piece of the game, coupled with an awareness of his patterns, that a victory was just

Preparation

around the corner. Alas, the victory that I so desired, continually eluded me, despite my best efforts. It was true that these were my best efforts, because, at the time, I simply did not see how I could do more. Then, the realization of that mirrored view came to me. The problem was simple. I hadn't yet fully put myself into the game. I never saw the vision of winning, and so, I couldn't fathom what that looked like. I remember the feeling when I closed my eyes, and in that moment, visualized the chess board in my mind. I was able to watch the pieces move across the board. I saw my grandfather's hand move the same piece, in the same way, and then it hit me. This was the first time that I was able to actually see myself playing the game.

We all know that many truly successfully athletes watch tapes of themselves playing their respective sport. They get to see where they made their mistakes, and how those around them did things differently to achieve victory. They can pause, rewind, and watch the same play over and over again. Clearly, we understand that when someone visualizes something, they are able to see it from more angles, and gain a greater perspective. Along with that, what truly breathes life into anything of meaning, and changes the fabric of that reality, is when the person is able to mentally place themselves in the picture, as an achiever of the thing they are going after. I was able to accomplish this very thing with chess, and found that when I applied all that I knew, with all the want to win I had beating right out of my chest, and I not only saw myself in the moment, but I placed myself in the winner's circle. I finally beat my grandfather. He and I continued for years to play, and I never lost a game again.

The reality that you can place yourself into the moment of success and achievement and have that always become the outcome would be misguided, of course. The real treasure and wisdom however is in the truth of belief in the concept of seeing yourself within something, and therefore having a greater awareness of what is involved. Adding that learned ability to the combination of your continued effort, personal skillset, heightened awareness, desire to win, and placement of yourself creating your masterpiece, breathes life into your situation and possesses the ability to ignite the flame of your vision.

When we expand our perception, our thoughts, our interpretations, and act on them, the possibilities are endless. It is inside that mindset that we take back control. We become shareholders again of own destiny, and allow ourselves to be in a place worthy of who we are designed to be; masters creating masterpieces.

Preparation

What if you decided it was time to create your masterpiece too?

Preparation

Preparation is a key component in creating your masterpiece. It is the first step to take before you do anything that you intend to do well. In the culinary world, there is a French term known as Mise en place, which translates loosely to everything in its place. This is an imperative part of the cooking process, yet it is so very simple. It is simply the act of being prepared to execute by ensuring that you have the tools and ingredients necessary for success in their proper position, and readily accessible to you.

There is, however, a preparation that comes before you get your tools and ingredients in place. It is impossible to know what ingredients you need without a recipe, and you can't have a recipe without visualizing what you want the end result to look like. This principle is true for the creation of any masterpiece. The initial preparation, begins with visualizing the final piece.

When you can conceive an idea of what the completion of your creation looks like, you can visualize yourself creating it, and this will allow you to prepare your path to success. Throughout this book, you will have multiple opportunities to take an introspective approach as you prepare to create your masterpiece.

Preparation

It is through the intentional reflection of our experiences that we are able to capture the insight which lies within those moments. Reflect on what you have just experienced in this chapter, find the insight that lives within it, and take this moment to press those insights to paper.

_____
_____
_____
_____
_____
_____
_____
_____
_____
_____
_____
_____
_____
_____

The Master Within

Sculpting: Sales

Sculpting and sales have quite a bit in common. When we think about it, both the sculptor and the sales professional have to begin with the end in mind. They both need to have certain characteristics, such as intestinal fortitude, vision, and self-awareness. The best in these categories have these characteristics and others, at very high levels.

What if you knew yourself? What if you really had the level of awareness that was so deep, it bred confidence at such a high level, that no one could tell you that you are anything different? Would you be empowered to strive where others may have fallen? Do you think that you would be able to hold on to that self-awareness when outside forces, even those closest to you, tried to get you to fulfill the potential that they see you as having? If you knew who you were, who would you be?

Michelangelo knew who he was. Today you can travel to Italy and see what is said to be some of the greatest fresco paintings this world has to offer. You can travel to the Sistine Chapel and St Peter's Basilica, and simply look up. As you gaze upon the brilliant work, you may know that it took Michelangelo four years to paint the Sistine Chapel. The world saw him as divine. When he was 13, Michelangelo convinced his father that grammar school was not where his time would be best spent. Instead, as the story goes, Michelangelo pled with his father so that he might have the opportunity to be an apprentice for Domenico Ghirlandaio, who was the most famous fresco painter in Italy at the time. Of course, his father conceded, and the world gets to have magnificent works of art as a result.

Sculpting from the mind of a painter; this is how others viewed Michelangelo's style when it came to statues. Michelangelo was quite guarded about his process, and wouldn't allow people to watch him plan or work. When the world saw him as a painter, or a painter with the ability to sculpt, Michelangelo considered himself a sculptor. He had vision, and the intestinal fortitude to see the process of creating marble masterpieces through. He had the ability to paint, we can see that plainly… but he also wrote poetry. Michelangelo knew himself enough to know who and what he was. He understood that though the folks from the outside looking in may have seen him as a painter who could sculpt, their perception did not alter his reality. In fact, he was so comfortable with himself that he took on works such as the Sistine chapel, that would perpetuate the belief of the masses.

Sometimes, when we are insecure about a thing, we avoid it. Sometimes if we see ourselves a certain way, we work so hard at adjusting the perception of the people looking at us, that we lose track of honing our craft. If we truly believe that each experience we have provides an opportunity for growth, then doesn't it make sense to seize as many of those opportunities as we can?

He understood that painting and poetry did not take away from his ability to sculpt. In fact, these alternate creative outlets may have enhanced them. We don't know that, but what we do know is that his tireless efforts to petition the right stone for his pieces sent him on trips back to Carrera, where he meticulously chose the perfect pieces in which to carve his visions and expose his brilliance to the world. His passion for his purpose was a consistent flame that was fueled with his intestinal fortitude. He was a true visionary.

In fact, his vision was so clear, that he was able to create one of the most significant works of art this world has seen, using a piece of stone that not one, but two other sculptors had previously deemed unusable. Let's take a moment here to rest in the magnitude of that statement. Two separate sculptors, who were known for sculpting, and seen as sculptors to the world, made attempts to create brilliant works of art with this huge piece of marble. Both of them decided that the stone was not capable of being turned into their visions for the stone. Then, one day, roughly 40 years after the stone was originally excavated, along comes a sculptor who the world sees as a painter with the ability to sculpt. Michelangelo takes on the challenge of this, previously deemed unworkable, stone and in about two year's time, he creates the David. The David! You know, that brilliant masterpiece that has been replicated time and again for the masses to have the ability to grasp just a piece of. This is how Giorgio Vasari introduced this work, "...*When all was finished, it cannot be denied that this work has carried off the palm from all other statues, modern or ancient, Greek or Latin; no other artwork is equal to it in any respect, with such just proportion, beauty and excellence...*". Could you imagine what this world would have missed out on, if Michelangelo would have simply conceded to the public view, and seen himself as a painter?

Zig Ziglar, who has often been referred to as the world's most popular motivational speaker, was known to the world as a speaker and an author. Before the world recognized him as such, Zig Ziglar was seen solely as a sales person. He was an excellent sales person! However, Zig Ziglar knew that he could write too.

The confidence Zig held in his capability to be an author was astounding. As we know, the first book Zig Ziglar ever wrote was rejected. It was rejected over and over again; to the tune of thirty-nine times! Thirty-nine times this man had to process the rejection of professionals of a field in which he was trying to establish himself. Some of us are hesitant to even speak to other humans, because we fear rejection. This man, kept going. He knew that the world needed what he had to contribute.

A small publishing company finally did pick up that book, in 1975, after some thirty other publishing companies said no. 'See You At The Top' which was the name of that book, went on to sell more than 250,000 copies, and is still selling today. At last count, the book has sold more than two million copies.

Could you imagine what would have happened if Zig Ziglar allowed other people's perception of him get in the way of the realization of himself?

Had Zig Ziglar accepted any of those rejections as a reflection of his ability, he may have stayed in sales, and had a comfortable life for himself. The acceptance of that rejection would have come at a tremendous cost to millions of people, that we can only begin to quantify now, because Zig Ziglar had the intestinal fortitude to pursue his vision and fuel his passion. If Zig Ziglar did not grind out the process of getting his first book published, then there is a real chance that this world would have missed out on his thirty-two other books. There is a strong possibility that the acceptance of rejection would have led to other failures in his life, and Zig Ziglar may never have become a speaker. The butterfly effect that could have occurred, is a little overwhelming when you think about it.

Millions of people would not have gotten to hear his message. The message that the world has proven it so desperately needed. What is the world waiting to get from you? What lives will your masterpiece impact?

Do you know yourself so well that your foundation can not be shaken?

Carve Out Your Path

Throughout this book, you will have many opportunities to personally take action, and implement patterns that will help you carve out your path, so that you can build the bridge between the art form and a life skill; and then, you will have the authority to walk across that bridge at your discretion.

This is about Developing a skill through measured intentional and strategic energy, effort and consistency. Any master we know of today did not begin by creating masterpieces. They developed their skills, and grew into who we now know them to be. So, if you are thinking that sales, or any tool, is simply not your thing, understand that it is fine to acknowledge where you believe yourself to be. You've got to know where you are in order to get where you're going.

Right now, you are going to take some time to reflect and to begin to ask yourself the below questions, then answer them to the fullest of your capability. After that, I want you to commit to performing one daily discipline.

Create Schedule and do Same activities
@ Same time 5 days/week

Keeping in mind that our strengths, when over-utilized, can develop into weaknesses, we must always take note of the weaknesses that play major roles in our shortcomings. In relation to sales, what are weaknesses are playing a major role in your shortcomings?

not making systems

The thing that remains standing, long after you've taken your final seat, is your legacy. So what do you want your legacy to say about you?

I helped people, made people feel good and helped to preserve and protect the planet.

What consistent actions can you perform to show people that you are trustworthy, you have empathy, and that you maintain high integrity?

Stay true to my word
do what I say
be on time
be honest

When you present great ideas with the hope of gaining buy in, and fail to obtain your desired results, what response would best prepare you for your next opportunity?

let's think about it some more

You may have noticed that we didn't discuss the steps to the sale, or how to close a prospect, or any of the general sales techniques when we spoke of someone who is highly regarded for his salesmanship. We did discuss the 39 rejections that he pushed through. We also discussed how his book sold more than 250,000 copies, and was a tremendous success. We went on to discuss how he could have resigned his position and continued life being comfortable and successful, but he chose the tough road.

You can have the best idea in the world, but if you haven't convinced yourself, you will not be able to convince someone else. It will not be until you sell yourself on the idea of your success that anyone else will be able to fully see it. What good does it do you to have something with the potential for greatness if it is not allowed to be great.

I would like for you to write down your biggest dream, your largest goal, the thing that you would consider to be your masterpiece. That's it - just write it down. Tomorrow, I will ask that you write it once more, and then tell yourself what you will do to celebrate that achievement. Each day after, for the next thirty days, just spend five minutes thinking about, planning out, and getting to the point of an action plan. Let's begin to carve out your path, shall we?

Sculpting: Sales

It is through the intentional reflection of our experiences that we are able to capture the insight which lies within those moments. Reflect on what you have just experienced in this chapter, find the insight that lives within it, and take this moment to press those insights to paper.

Top producing listing agent that provides a top quality product & experience. My reputation is golden. I have a team working for me and we are transforming the way people experience real estate while protecting the planet for future generations.

The Master Within

Painting: Leadership

When we look at painting, and consider all that is involved with regard to creating the final work, we can see clearly that both painting and leadership require much of the artist. You see, putting your mark on someone, much like putting paint on canvas, requires time, consistency, vision, effort, and patience. Just as paint can enhance, ruin, or fully transform many different surfaces, so too can leadership enhance, diminish, or transform many different types of people.

Pablo Picasso communicated this correlation beautifully when he said, "Every act of creation, is first of all, an act of destruction." When we think about this truth, and we understand that before we can create something, we must first destroy something, we can really wrap our minds around what it takes to access our inner master. It Is in that realization that you can create your masterpiece.

Just as you must destroy minerals to make pigment for paint, you must also destroy obstacles to create the followers that you will lead. We break to build. This doesn't necessarily mean we break others, or even ourselves (though sometimes we must). We must break poor mindsets. We break the restrictions we have inadvertently placed on ourselves. We break the idea that we are not all masters in our own right, and then, we build our masterpieces.

The discipline that it takes to be a great painter, is not light work by any means. Nor should it be said that the discipline of a great leader is anything to scoff at. Consistency is key, perseverance is necessary, then growth can become inevitable. These things are true, if you are going to execute to either art masterfully. The weight of the want behind these masters, is the momentum they use to propel themselves into their next steps. The accountability which comes with the understanding that if one is to create anything, first, something must be broken... it is, understandably so, enough to entice someone to stagnate and choose not to create.

Painting: Leadership

The good news is that you have a choice. You can choose to become overwhelmed by the realization, or you can choose to respect the magnitude of the position, and acknowledge your personal capabilities. You see, if we can believe that the meek will inherit the earth, then we must consider our role. To be meek is not to be weak. In fact, those things are quite the opposite. It takes real strength to know your place, in a given situation, and in life. A part of knowing your place is understanding the impact of your role.

Some people understand their role, and have a long-term vision for their life that is accurate. Others think they know what they want to do, and realize later that, either things changed, a greater awareness of the position led them to know that it was not for them, or circumstances changed and they found a different passion… a new calling. It doesn't matter if you knew who you wanted to be when you were five, or found out when you turned fifty… all that will matter is that you take the time to know.

As we know, Picasso completed his first painting at the age of nine. This painting led to almost two thousand others, with at least one piece, named Garson a La Pipe, selling for more than one hundred million dollars! We also know that he created more than 30 masterpieces (you can find a list of them on pablopicasso.org).

It has been estimated that Picasso, who died at the age of ninety-one, produced somewhere around fifty thousand pieces! That number would be inclusive of somewhere around twelve thousand drawings with fewer than two-thousand of those pieces being paintings. This world-renowned painter, who was clearly a creator, made close to fifty thousand pieces, and less than five percent of the art he created were paintings. How then, could he be considered a painter?

Let's look at his masterpieces. Les Femmes d'Alger, for example, became the most expensive piece of art ever sold at auction, and is said to have gone for more than one hundred and seventy million dollars. The auction site casually tweeted about it on Twitter on May 11, 2015. The remaining thirty-two pieces were all paintings. So, yes, he was an artist, he was a creator, but at his core, he was a painter. He knew this. Picasso embraced this, and he knew real success as a result of knowing who he was, understanding his potential impact, and executing with excellence.

I believe that because he knew who he was, and accepted the magnitude of his position, that he was able to consistently put in the time that it took to execute his visions with excellence. As his confidence grew, so too did his creativity, which ultimately translated to a momentum so fierce that it would only be stopped by death. We know this to be true, because we know that he was working on his self-portrait, which was titled, "Self Portrait Facing Death" until three o'clock in the morning, on the day that he died.

Some choose to go softly into the night. Others decide to let their passion fuel them, so that they can shine their dimming light, until there is no place left for their flame.

Just as this brilliant painter used the layers of paint, brushstroke, by brushstroke to create dignity, depth, and a level of beauty that the world still longs to see, so too does John Maxwell use his talents as an expert in leadership, to make the world a brighter, more beautiful place.

People travel from all over the world to hear John speak. They make decisions to change their lives dramatically, as a result of having been influenced by someone with whom they may never get to have a one-on-one conversation. Can you imagine making a major life decision, as a result of hearing someone that you may never get to know? Millions have, and it is probably safe to say that millions more will.

This is not a bad thing, when you are following the right leader. The truth is that John understands leadership at such a high level, that he figured out how to lead millions of people, and he even found a way to be an integral part in growing them into becoming better versions of themselves, and, as a result, better leaders for others. He has done so, without having a single one-on-one conversation with most of the people he has influenced. He made a connection without using a traditional method of connecting. He continues to successfully do so to this day.

With more than twenty million copies of his books sold, you might say he has had an impact. Some of those books have been translated to more than fifty different languages, so it is pretty clear that he has had an impact that is worldwide. This is no small feat, and this is simply the tip of the iceberg when you dig into all of the influencing this leader has done.

He did not start off on his journey with status and wealth. Nor did he have a steady platform. So, if you are thinking that you need status to influence others, then I am here to tell you that if you take the time to make a positive impact on enough people, you will get the status you need to be able to share your masterpiece with even more. It will be your passion that fuels your intestinal fortitude, and your intestinal fortitude that feeds your drive and your drive that will determine your success.

John Maxwell is quoted as having said, "You see, my passion in life is growing and equipping others to do remarkable things and lead significant and fulfilled lives." To accomplish this, he had to find the best, most effective way for him to be able to share his passion with the world. There is no limit to the number of people John intends to equip, influence, or impact. When he looked at who he was, and began to understand what his strengths were, it was then, in his growing self-awareness, that he was able to make a decision… not just a decision, but an informed decision that would radically transform millions of lives, including his own.

Art has a tendency to inspire. It pulls out emotions, draws people in, and communicates universally in its own language. A language that speaks clearly enough for people across the world to listen to and interpret, based on their mindset, beliefs, and world views. Regardless of whether a piece brings one to tears, joy, or simply has them stop in their place in awe of the work; art often speaks to people. Art has the ability to influence people.

Art has the ability to impact people enough to create a fundamental change within.

For me, leadership is an art form. I believe that real leaders help to create and grow other leaders. I believe that helping someone realize their potential is one of the most important things a leader can do. Someone who chooses to follow, is putting themselves in a vulnerable position. They are extending trust, showing restraint, and allowing themselves to be subject to judgement by someone in whom the follower sees tremendous value. So much so, that the follower risks their reputation, they risk their self-image, they risk their dignity to become the canvas for an artist who chose to have them be a part of their work.

When you dig deep within, and discover the reasons you do what you do, you can find the core of what really motivates you. It is in your motivation that you can discover your passion. If you are to fuel your, much needed, intestinal fortitude, then I am urging you to find your passion. Write it down, in places that you are sure to see it. Meditate on who you are and what you are called for, for at least fifteen minutes each day. Do not allow this call to action overwhelm you. You don't need to start with fifteen minutes a day, but you do need to start with the end in mind.

Painting: Leadership

APPLY THE BRUSHSTROKES

Why do you do what you do?

_____

_____

_____

_____

Do you enjoy what you are doing, or wish you were doing something else?

_____

_____

_____

_____

If you could only do one thing for the rest of your life, what would it be, and why?

_____

_____

_____

_____

What are three things in your life that bring you undeniable joy?

_____

_____

_____

_____

Remember your action plan. Meditate every day. Find a quiet space, and it does not matter if you start with1 minute, 5 minutes, or 15 minutes. Just get to the 15-minute mark, and stay there consistently. This will help you apply the brushstrokes to your chosen canvas, as you paint out the vision of your masterpiece in your mind.

Painting: Leadership

It is through the intentional reflection of our experiences that we are able to capture the insight which lies within those moments. Reflect on what you have just experienced in this chapter, find the insight that lives within it, and take this moment to press those insights to paper.

_____

_____

_____

_____

_____

_____

_____

_____

_____

_____

_____

_____

The Master Within

Comedy: Communication

What if you knew the thing that drove you? Would you be able to share your vision with those around you? Do you think that you have an idea of who you are and what you want to do, but when you communicate your vision and goals to others, the message doesn't seem to get through? Could you stand in a crowded room, with loads of people standing, and staring in a moment of hushed anticipation, and tell them who you are, what you love, how why and what you intend to do? Could you get your message out to a single person, making it so clear that they become filled with passion for your purpose?

Sometimes, we know who we are. Sometimes we know what we want to do. Sometimes we have lots of tools at the ready, that we intend to use to share our masterpiece with the world. Like a good comedian, who has a rough night... the timing isn't always appropriate. Or maybe the delivery just isn't there, when we go to pitch our passion. If we glance into the artistry behind the world of comedy, we can see that comedy and communication coincide.

Jerry Seinfeld, is known as a master of his craft. We can see that he has been highly recognized, awarded multiple times, and has had what many would consider to be a highly lucrative career. These intentional wins are not simply a result of having a natural talent. They are more likely a result of a winning formula compiled of things like diligence, practice, consistency, and intentionality.

To learn comedic timing, is more like refining a skill. To master the gestures, pair those with the right words, and pause when appropriate, is an art. One of the reasons that Seinfeld is considered one of the top one hundred comedians of all time, is because he has a relentless level of consistency with regard to his process. He consistently practices his craft. He regularly reviews and revises his jokes.

Seinfeld is quite intentional with each placement of the words he uses, and each breath, pause, or gesture made. He can be so intentional, because he dissects his sets. He tears them down and builds them up again, over and over, both in his mind and in real time. The smaller crowds tend to provide the most criticism for a comedian. Because he knows this to be true, Jerry Seinfeld continues to frequent the kind of establishments that cater to fewer people. He spends time looking for honest feedback, in a world that allows him to surround himself with false praise.

Consider who you would seek out if you had a net worth of more than nine-hundred million dollars. Would you look for ways to keep improving, or would you rest in your success?

It could be said that Jerry Seinfeld changed the relationship that viewers have with stand-up comedians. If we consider how many episodes were played, then it is safe to say that the fictional character that Jerry Seinfeld created and also played, as the star of his show, Seinfeld, is the most watched stand-up comedian in our history to date. By being true to himself, true to his calling, and by understanding that when you stop growing, you start dying; Seinfeld received a platform which has allowed him to communicate to the world.

His ability to move a crowd likely played a huge role in providing the confidence necessary to convince producers to see his vision for the show. Had he not been able to communicate his vision, he would have been the only one capable of seeing it. Now, a world without the television show is not the end of the world. Yet, the impact one has should not always be measured by lack of devastation to the whole world. While it is true that comedy would have gone on with or without Seinfeld; I believe it is safe to say that Jerry Seinfeld sharing his masterpiece with the world is better than him having kept it to himself.

If we understand communication to be the act of transferring information through acts of verbal messages, by way of the written word, and/or non-verbal signals; then we know that words are not merely heard. Actions are interpreted, body language is analyzed (often times on a conscious and subconscious level), tonality is considered, and words are processed. Words matter. What you say or write, those things are important. As much as words matter, it is important to remember that all of the communication matters. We can not use an aggressive face and yell harshly words of encouragement, and then expect the person on the receiving end to be able to fully accept those words in a positive light.

Comedy: Communication

Our intentions are judged by perceptions. If we are perceived as an angry person, then even in our expressions of joy, people will be more prone to judge it as anger. If we are seen as hyper-critical, then when we try to help, the alternate party will likely start out on the defensive side. When we understand our audience, and we communicate to them on a level that speaks most effectively to them, we are in a position to better hear and be heard.

When we consider one of the greatest communicators of his time, Martin Luther King Jr., what do we see? We see cadence. We see discipline. We see structure. We see flow. We see body language… We see the same winning formula in the master of this craft, as we do the master of comedy.

As we consider the speech that epitomized Dr. King, we know that even though he had the speech, in its entirety, written down, he rarely referenced his notes, and did not look at his paper at all after the eleven- minute mark. His speech was brilliantly comprised of what I visualize as puzzle pieces of moments from speeches and sermons that he had strung together over twenty years of creating. This masterpiece was a verbal mosaic of years of experience, played out with the body language of a seasoned communicator, and delivered with the cadence of an orator so brilliant that he drew millions to a movement in a time when the nation urged them to stand still.

Dr. King had a vision, and he honed his craft, and developed a way to communicate his vision in a way that would not only impact a nation, but also expanded globally. The 'I Have A Dream' speech is one that is still relevant, still impactful, and still moving. It is a true masterpiece, by a disciplined, consistent, master of communication.

"The question is not if we will be extremists, but what kind of extremists we will be. Will we be extremists for hate or love?" This, one of many brilliant statements by Dr. King, signifies who he was, and what kind of vision he had. This was a time that required the approach of an extremist. Dr. King knew that his audience was frustrated. He knew that the people to whom he was speaking, they were at a crossroads, with a real choice to make.

Because of his ability to communicate, Dr. King was able to inspire a nation. At a time where many saw violence as the only option, he was able to guide the masses down an alternate path. We know that he was able to help advance civil rights through non-violent acts, using his Christian beliefs and the non-violent activism of Mahatma Ghandi as inspiration.

When he spoke, people listened. We know that Dr. King was not the first to speak out or speak up. We know that others before him tried to influence our nation, and attempted to create their own civil rights movement. We also know, that no one was able to garner the reach that Dr. King commanded. The respect he earned, and trust that he built forged an army who willingly marched on his command.

The cadence with which one speaks, the timing of delivery and considered pauses, the movements they choose to make with their bodies and faces… the daily discipline of practicing, studying, reading, writing and doing whatever it takes to hone their skills… these consistent acts of executing allows growth. The repetition may seem redundant, but when communication is smooth, we don't always think about what it took to get it there. We sometimes find too much comfort in a moment of success, and that may cause us to elongate our period of rest. It is important to mark your wins. Holding onto them in moments of doubt can help you get out of whatever funk you may find yourself in. Do you want to win once, or over and over again?

PERFECT PRACTICE

I am certain that we have all heard that practice makes perfect. The confusion behind that is, to me, the statement seems to be an abbreviated way to say that practice makes permanent, and perfect practice makes perfect permanent. What if we are practicing incorrectly? When we practice, we are essentially creating a habit. Isn't it so important to invest the extra energy and effort to ensure that the habit you are forming is as close to perfect as it can be?

Take a few moments to answer these questions honestly, and following the questions, execute to your consistent discipline with excellence.

Comedy: Communication

Understanding the multiple aspects of communication, knowing that the majority of what is being communicated is interpreted by means beyond the verbal impact; What are three things you can do today to communicate more effectively?

_____

_____

_____

_____

_____

When you have a vision that you want to share, what are steps that you could take to ensure that you are communicating your vision effectively to the audience of choice? What can you do to have your vision more clearly seen by others?

_____

_____

_____

_____

_____

What are you doing right now that is effective, consistent, and would be considered as your communication strengths?

_____

_____

_____

_____

_____

Practice communicating with people. Take your weaknesses and really focus on them. If eye contact is your issue, then focus on saying hello to everyone you come into contact with, have a smile on your face, and hold eye contact until they pass you. If body language is an issue, practice your body language while you are on the phone with people, but do so in front of a mirror, so that you can see yourself.

Do not be afraid to get honest feedback from people you trust. A part of growing is having awareness. Remember, when you are receiving that feedback, that they are not being critical of you, they are simply participating in your growth and success.

Above all else, if there is one thing you can practice perfectly right away, it is to listen with the intent to learn, not with intent to respond. When you really listen to people, it matters. They feel valued, and they begin to value you at a different level.

It is through the intentional reflection of our experiences that we are able to capture the insight which lies within those moments. Reflect on what you have just experienced in this chapter, find the insight that lives within it, and take this moment to press those insights to paper.

_____

_____

_____

_____

_____

_____

_____

_____

_____

_____

_____

_____

_____

_____

Comedy: Communication

Acting: Influence

Tom Hanks is known for saying that acting is a never-ending process of examining where you are in life. Knowing who you are will always impact your ability to influence those who you are with. If you can not influence, you will not lead. It is as simple as that.

When we look at acting, it is not difficult to acknowledge the craft as an art. It is, in fact, a performance art. An art compiled of movement, intonations, and gestures. These things brought together effectively, have the ability to transport the viewer into the world of a fictional character. It is a unique position to be in, having the ability to evoke real emotion regarding a fictional character. When someone makes the choice to become a method actor, such as Tom

Hanks, that person must allow them self to be engulfed in the role. Essentially, there is a commitment to become the character.

Becoming the character requires commitment, at a VERY high level. You (meaning the person who committed to becoming the character) commit to growing beyond your comfort zone, and you step into the world of someone else. The way in which you speak, how you move, and all of the little idiosyncratic traits that make up the role, you adopt and develop. You grow them until they become this completely new character, and then you perform as that character. This process can take months or even years to achieve.

Tom Hanks has been able to achieve it brilliantly time and time again. The sheer strength of mind that it takes to succumb to such a role, and somehow not lose yourself in the process is impressive. Acting, like most things, requires full commitment. If actors can spend months researching a role, learning body movements, gaining new skills, and speaking another language to play a role for a movie; imagine what you could do if you spent an extra fifteen minutes a day focused on you.

What would you learn about yourself if you focused on yourself? What would you grow about yourself, if you gave yourself the permission to do it? The discipline it takes to focus on growing one's self might be as difficult as it is to temporarily become someone else. The truth here is that sometimes it is easier to be someone else. Sometimes putting on a show it more comfortable than having our true selves exposed. People want to be liked. People want to be needed and wanted. As far as I am concerned, these things are simply in our human make up.

So, if we know there is no avoiding it, we might as well face it… head on. Tom Hanks doesn't get lost in a role, because he knows who he is. He didn't get consumed with the drugs along the journey, or the Hollywood stigmas, because he accepts who he is. You can know yourself, accept yourself, love yourself, and still grow yourself. This is not an either-or type of situation. You can see your flaws and love yourself. You can turn potential into performance. You can accept who you are, and still get better! Hear this, you can accept who you are, and still get better.

"Action seems to follow feeling, but really action and feeling go together; and by regulating the action, which is under the more direct control of the will, we can indirectly regulate the feeling, which is not." – **Dale Carnegie**

Influence is imperative for success. If you can not influence yourself, you will not influence others in the way that you desire. Sometimes, in order to influence a feeling, we must first influence the action; as noted above in the popular Dale Carnegie quote. Your ability to influence, will impact your ability to help others.

Creating a masterpiece that you plan to keep in the closet tucked away from the world… that is an injustice to the world. Can you justify putting in the time, energy, and effort? Can you picture yourself performing at your highest capacity? What if no one ever got to experience the light you shine so bright? In a world filled with darkness, you have a light. Your ability to have influence will determine who gets to see that light.

Influence is not simply power. In fact, a simple search on your favorite search engine will bring up several similar definitions of the word. They will all be comparable to this; Influence is the ability to have an effect on the character, development, or behavior of someone or something, or the effect itself. That sounds a lot like leadership to me. If you can not lead yourself, then it is likely a fair statement to say that you should not lead anyone else. The same too can apply for influence.

Acting: Influence

Dale Carnegie is known for his self-improvement courses, and his very popular book entitled, 'How to Win Friends and Influence People'. He understood early on that influence impacts outcomes. The more people he got to know, like, and trust him, equated to the more he was able to influence the people. His versatility led to tremendous capabilities, because he impacted millions with his work. His work remains popular to this day, and he passed away in 1955.

He understood that the way we think matters. He understood that how we communicate matters. Dale Carnegie understood how to touch people, without ever having put a hand on them. Almost like a virtual hug, without the emoji to communicate that action.

There are four ways, and only four ways, in which we have contact with the world. We are evaluated and classified by these four contacts: what we do, how we look, what we say, and how we say it. **– Dale Carnegie**

Just as in acting, and influencing… in life, your presentation matters. The way you carry yourself, the way you lean in when you are listening… even the way you shake a hand or give a hug. The words you choose will always matter, the way in which they hear you will matter more.

CONTROL YOUR NARRATIVE

The truth is that every person has their own story. The person who tells your story will control your narrative. Being influential is a skill that can be dressed up to look like a natural talent. Having very intentional actions will help to hone this skill.

Are you so passionate about your position, and so open and honest with people, that you find them choosing to adopt your views?

_____

_____

_____

_____

_____

ACTING: INFLUENCE

In times where influence is necessary, do you find yourself forcing the point until the person concedes to your view point?

_____

_____

_____

_____

_____

Do you see yourself as the smartest person in the room at any given time?

_____

_____

_____

_____

_____

What do you think about when you have down time? Are you focused on the tasks of the day, planning for tomorrow, or trying to remember something you've forgotten?

_____

_____

_____

_____

_____

How much time do you spend reflecting on yourself and your day each day?

_____

_____

_____

_____

_____

Acting: Influence

Who do you most want to influence right now? Why? What one thing could you adjust that would impact your influence with them?

_____

_____

_____

_____

_____

People pick up on actions that are not genuine. As a whole, humans generally want to surround themselves with honest, loyal, caring people. They want to matter, be treated with respect, and be shown grace. As you interact with people, make a mental note of how they perceive their interactions with you. Do they feel like you genuinely care for them? Consider how you can show them that you believe they matter.

The Master Within

It is through the intentional reflection of our experiences that we are able to capture the insight which lies within those moments. Reflect on what you have just experienced in this chapter, find the insight that lives within it, and take this moment to press those insights to paper.

_____

_____

_____

_____

_____

_____

_____

_____

_____

_____

_____

_____

_____

Acting: Influence

Photography: Mindset

What if perspective was everything? You may already know, I believe that a key component to success is execution. What if I told you that without accounting for perspective, it is difficult to implement a process. Our perspective is like the lens through which we see the world. Are you committed to controlling your perspective?

In this famous quote by Annie Leibovitz, "The first thing I did with my very first camera was climb Mt. Fuji. Climbing Mt. Fuji is a lesson in determination and moderation. It would be fair to ask if I took the moderation part to heart. But it certainly was a lesson in respecting your camera. If I was going to live with this thing, I was going to have to think about what that meant. There were not going to be any pictures without it." We can plainly see her passion and dedication. She had a grasp, early on, of the magnitude of the task at hand. She knew her passion, and committed to execute to her vision to see it through. But first, it is as though she decided she would test herself. Getting a clear view of her intestinal fortitude, she began to understand different layers of herself. It takes self-awareness to grow. It is quite difficult to understand who you are going to be, if you do not have a grasp on who you've become.

Annie is an American portrait photographer. While she is known for having photographed John Lennon on the day that he passed away, she was also the lead photographer for Rolling Stone magazine. She was also the first woman to have her collection exhibited at the National Portrait Gallery in Washington, DC.

She is known for capturing images that were later deemed as iconic and controversial. She has photographed celebrities, and became known for having her sitters (the subjects that she would photograph) become very involved in her work.

The lighting, the lens, the angle of the shot, the subject in question, and the scene... these are big picture details that get captured in the flash of a bulb. The vision that she has for each subject is carried out and communicated through her set and the lens. The angle impacts the perspective, so simply standing in a single location taking a standard photograph, is not likely the vision that comes to mind, when you imagine an artist such as this. I imagine fluid motion. I see twists and turns of the photographer's body. In my mind, it is easy to visualize her squatting down, stretching her body to its capacity, or even climbing to higher ground in order to get her shot… something that can also be described as, making her vision clear to the world.

Sometimes, in order to get the full picture, we have to adjust our angle of perspective. Have you ever stood at the edge of a lake or the sea, and gazed in awe at the reflection of the sun, sky and trees? When you look down while in that standing position, you can even see a reflection of yourself. All of that surface-view is great, but what if you want to go deeper? If you are interested in seeing the fish swimming in the lake, then you are not going to be likely to do so, just by looking down on the water. Instead, kneel down, and get to an angle that allows you to see beneath the surface without physically getting in or going under water. With the right angle, you can see through, straight across, under the surface of the water. With that new perspective, you can see the rocks, the fish swimming, and even get a glimpse of their world, by simply being flexible enough to adjust your position to improve your perception.

There is value in knowing not only what your perspective is, but also how it impacts what you see. There is tremendous value in understanding how and when to change that perspective. I believe that Annie understands herself enough to know that sometimes she needs to have the flexibility to view things from alternate angles. It is in that flexibility that you will truly see your subject, and be able to best create your body of work.

It is probably safe to say that Tony Robbins has strategically made a career that is centered around mindset management. Considering the trials in his youth that he has expressed as having, it is easy to see how he might have fallen into a self-deprecating mindset. He lacked parental stability as a child, and is known for having had a chaotic and abusive home life. We know that he left that home at the age of seventeen and did not return. It is also common knowledge that he did not get a college education. Yet today, he has an estimated net worth of somewhere near the five-hundred-million-dollar mark. He has written multiple books, and holds seminars regularly.

I believe that one's mindset truly impacts the way a person thinks. Those thoughts impact interpretation, communication, and ultimately, actions. Someone's mindset dynamically impacts their day, week, and ultimately, the direction of one's life. Hard work, consistency, a never-stop spirit, and the right mindset seem to be common threads in the lives of those who are often times considered to be lucky, or someone who is seen to be the person who seems to get the big breaks in life. Luck is not something we seem to be able to have control over, but our mindset, effort, and intestinal fortitude are things within our control. What if luck really had nothing to do with our good fortune? What if, however, we walked with favor from a loving God, received good will from those around us, surrounded ourselves with folks who love, support, and genuinely enjoy seeing us succeed. What if we controlled our mindset, so much so, that our preparation was at such a high level, on such a consistent basis, that it put us in position to not only be able to identify, but to also seize an opportunity before that opportunity were to pass beyond our reach? If we control our mindset, we control our journey. If we control our journey, then we determine our destination.

Understanding that humans are creatures of habit, we understand that it is imperative for us to create healthy habits. When we listen to the self-talk, you know those statements we make to ourselves when we react to a situation, what do we hear? If you have a mindset of growth and abundance, then you may tend to have more grace with yourself. Your words are likely to be something you might expect to hear from a supportive friend. When you make a mistake, you may tell yourself to get as much data from the experience as possible, so that when the opportunity presents itself again, you can be better prepared to succeed.

All too often, when speaking with people, I find that instead of giving themselves grace, they speak to themselves more like an abusive authority figure might. I have found that often times, when people correct themselves, they do so in just, such a negative way. Instead of finding the good and trying to grow, they focus on why they shouldn't have even made the attempt in the first place. Telling themselves things like they were dumb for even thinking they had a chance to succeed. I hear people call themselves idiots, and demonize their own attempts to stretch themselves or grow themselves. It's really unfortunate, and a rather saddening to experience.

Because we are creatures of habit, our self-talk becomes our perception of ourselves, and the world. It impacts the way we hear others, the way we perceive their communication, and the way we see ourselves. We have to control the narrative in our heads, because even if we can find ways to get past our self-destructive talk; it will leach out into how we communicate with others. Your mindset determines your destiny. So, all that's left is for you to decide where you want to go.

KEEP YOUR VISION IN FOCUS

Now is a great time to apply the skills discussed in the book thus far, and consider our application of them to this point. When you review the self-work portions of this book, do you approach them with a mindset of growth? Are you putting in the work? Have you written it off completely, or maybe this is your first read through, and you intend to work at the action items on your second read.

Whatever your approach has been to this point, remember that you can get so much more out of anything that you put your everything into. So, take a moment and check your progress. If you are on track, keep going! If you are off track, it is not too late to course correct. You are in control here, and you get to decide what you are going to get out of this.

When you approach a challenge, does your inner voice assume your success or does it focus solely on the challenges?

_____

_____

_____

_____

_____

When you hear criticism, do you interpret it as you lacking in ability, or do you see them as signals to adjust and increase your performance?

_____

_____

_____

_____

_____

How could you remind yourself of your past accomplishments when you feel discouraged, and use them to keep forward momentum?

_____

_____

_____

_____

_____

What are five things that other people say they love about you?

_____

_____

_____

_____

_____

What are five things that you love about yourself?

_____

_____

_____

_____

_____

If you had to change one thing that you say to yourself regularly, or that you do not say to yourself enough, what would it be?

_____

_____

_____

_____

You are enough. Whatever trials you come up against, whatever obstacle comes your way, remember… you are enough.

The Master Within

It is through the intentional reflection of our experiences that we are able to capture the insight which lies within those moments. Reflect on what you have just experienced in this chapter, find the insight that lives within it, and take this moment to press those insights to paper.

Photography: Mindset

Sports: Teamwork

What would you be able to accomplish if you never lost courage in moments that require risk to be taken? Who would you impact?

As an activist, a philanthropist, and someone who is regarded as one of the most significant and celebrated sports figures of our time; Muhammad Ali knew what it meant to take risks. He understood he had to develop a process of calculating his risks, so that he could be best prepared to execute to his decision. His willingness to take those risks are what led to, among other accolades, him earning three world championship belts, an Olympic gold medal, and victory in fifty-six of his sixty-one bouts. He publicly stood up for his beliefs, and used his fame as a sounding board to speak out against things he felt needed change. When he was diagnosed with Parkinson's disease, he did not throw in the towel. He used his influence, and he helped to raise forty-five million dollars toward the cause.

Ali is known for having said that service to others is the rent that you pay for your room here on Earth. He lived those words out through his philanthropic contributions. His philanthropy was not limited to impact locally. Understanding that he had a global platform, Muhammad Ali committed to maintaining a positive global impact. As with most things, in this too, his efforts were successful. So much so, that in nineteen ninety-eight, Ali was named as the United Nations messenger of peace.

We know that Muhammad Ali has been ranked as the best heavyweight boxer in history… In history! That is a huge statement, and it is one that has been evaluated and made by various boxing authorities. By his own account, Muhammad Ali was known to "float like a butterfly, and sting like a bee." This was a concise and brilliant communication about his boxing style. Muhammad Ali was a heavyweight who was able to move more like a lightweight.

Of course, we all know that footwork, while it is a big part of the picture, alone it will not create the greatest heavyweight in history. In addition to his fancy footwork, Muhammad Ali was known for adopting a pattern of boxing behaviors that were considered to be extremely high-risk maneuvers. He would do things like hold his hands by his sides, and I am not saying he had his hands down a bit. This man committed, and had his hands down so far that they were at his waist. Could you imagine being in a boxing ring with a noted heavyweight fighter and, at any point in that fight, decide to drop your hands and attempt to avoid being hit by moving your head backwards? That took commitment and confidence.

Muhammad Ali was very rarely the aggressor in his matches. He used the opportunities presented in his matches by capitalizing on the aggression of his opponents. The methods he used were definitely unorthodox, and of such high-risk, that they would lure his opponents into making mistakes. Those mistakes were opportunities that Ali regularly saw and seized.

He took risks that others were not able to take. They could not take those risks because they were not willing to suffer the repercussions that came, should they discover the risk to be miscalculated. Not only was Muhammad Ali willing to endure any negative impact of a miscalculated risk, but even when he took a hit, he maintained the confidence to do it again. Muhammad Ali was known for his ability to take a "punch" both in and out of the ring, but giving up was not in his bag of options from which to choose.

Muhammad Ali gave himself the fuel his confidence needed, long before he had anything to be confident about. He is known for having regularly called himself the greatest before he became the greatest. He spoke his reality, and then he used that self-boost to fuel his passion. You see, potential that has not yet been transformed into performance doesn't have much impact. It takes a lot to turn that potential into performance, and part of that process is going to involve taking some hits. Muhammad Ali knew how important it was to lift himself up.

I am here to tell you that your masterpiece deserves to be created. Do not hinder that effort by hitting yourself. Your ego will take many blows. There will be enough criticism, negative talk, and judgement from others along your journey. You should not be in the line of people who are against you. You've got to guard your self-talk, and control the conversations in your head. If you tell yourself that you are a failure, then how does that translate into fuel for success? It feeds negativity, and your tank needs to fill with hope, joy, and a positive self-image. Those positive things will help combat the irrational negative views that the world tries to convince you to have. And guess what, those negative views are not true. You matter. You have value. You are not a failure. You are not your mistakes. So, do not let anyone tell you otherwise, especially you.

I am not telling you that you are perfect. That would be silly and untrue. I am telling you to embrace your failures. Get back up from the fall, because that is when you build the most strength. In the moments of exhaustion, you are simply building endurance, so push on, press on, and keep on. You are worth fighting for. Your dream is worth building the endurance necessary to create your masterpiece.

Not all of the voices that surround you will be negative, though some days it may feel that way. If you focus on the voice inside of you, keeping it positive, motivating, and competitive, then you can be better equipped to handle criticism. You are in control of your destiny, and you get to decide which internal voice gets to speak the loudest, so choose wisely.

Derek Jeter, who is my favorite baseball player, was able to control his self-image through all of the years that led to him becoming a New York Yankee. His foundation was one of such strength that it was not broken, or even cracked, by the intense pressure that comes with playing on the Yankees. He knew who he was, and still does. He spent time developing his values, and decided that his character was one of the highest priorities for his legacy.

Jeter was and is a great leader, because he is a great teammate. In his time on the team, the Yankees gave him the nickname of Captain. He embodied professionalism, teamwork, and dedication. Derek Jeter is known as having the belief that others may be more talented than you are, but there is no excuse for anyone to work harder than you do. That is because he understands that talent alone will never win a world series.

Teamwork plays a major role in life. We can look at the game of baseball and watch how every player, while they have their individual statistics, is simply an integral piece to a puzzle that can display a picture of success or failure. The game is so team-centered, that if a batter hits a ball and the guy on third runs to home, but the original batter gets out, the hit counts as an earned run in, and the out does not go against their batting average. The rules influence the motivation of the individual to display a team-first mentality.

This is exactly the player that Derek Jeter embodied. He was about team above self. He loves the sport of baseball so much that he put the sport above himself also. When the entire sport of baseball took a major blow at the hand of the series of steroid scandals, Jeter never came under fire for any wrong doings, because he had made conscious, consistent, career decisions to rise above the temptations. Moreover, he helped the sport maintain a hope for its future integrity, by being such an asset and choosing to never take the easy route.

When people speak of him, Derek Jeter is held in high regard. He is someone who puts his team first. He is willing to sacrifice his body for plays. He has never been seen complaining about his contract, nor have we heard him threaten to go to a different team. His loyalty was made clear, and then he did what he said he would do... time and time again.

So, whether it is bunting a ball and eating an out, so he can reposition the man on first and second base, or sustaining legitimate injuries by diving head first into the stands so that he could catch a ball; Derek Jeter embodies the type of teammate any team would hope to have. He is never noted as being boastful, nor do you hear him speaking ill of other players in order to lift himself up.

Humility matters, even when you are the best. Whatever the thing is that you are best at, that thing does not define you… your character does. Character is who you are when no one is looking. It is the core of your truest self. With all of the golden gloves and championship rings, Derek Jeter may be seen as someone who has good cause to be boastful, yet his humility speaks to his class. His willingness to do what it takes, to never make excuses, to hold himself and his team accountable, and to be the example are what make his legacy shine the most, to me.

Of course, you need to remind yourself of the things that you are great at, and remember of what you are capable. Your accomplishments need to be enjoyed, and your successes noted. Then, it is time to get better, do better, and be better. Life is a continued cycle of growth and obstacles. While Muhammad Ali believed that the mountain you have to climb wouldn't be the thing to tire you, because it would be the pebble in your shoe… I agree with that statement, and also believe that you should take note of the mountain too. If you do not have the mental fortitude necessary to press on, the world may never get to experience what you have to offer.

Your confidence will allow you to take risks. Your humility will allow you to grow from any missed calculations. This journey into your individual artistry will not be an easy one. You will have moments, maybe hours, or possibly even days that string together and are consumed with thoughts of giving in or giving up, when they once were focused on pushing through. This is not an 'if' statement, but rather a 'when' statement. So, please remember this; when you feel like throwing in the towel, you are simply building stamina. Just take that towel, use it for its intended purpose, which is not to be thrown in, but rather to wipe the sweat off your brow, and push on.

MAINTAIN THE ENDURANCE TO WIN

Nothing big happens in single day. Things more often take consistency, time, effort, and a relentless pursuit. Building your endurance makes a difference, it will be maintaining that endurance that impacts the outcome. Knowing your strengths can help you improve your weaknesses. Being confident and being arrogant are different. Go through this next set of questions, then reflect and focus on what it will take you to get through the storms that are likely to come.

What makes you a great teammate?

_____
_____
_____
_____
_____

Sports: Teamwork

What are your strongest skills? How can you use them to develop those around you?

_____

_____

_____

_____

If you had to choose two things you would improve about yourself, what would they be?

_____

_____

_____

_____

_____

If today, you found out that you had exactly one year to develop your legacy, what would you do first to ensure you effectively impact what people remember about you?

_____
_____
_____
_____
_____

In your toughest times, your darkest moments, what can you do to get yourself to take the next step?

_____
_____
_____
_____
_____

Sports: Teamwork

How many people are you committed to helping this week? This month? This year?

_____

_____

_____

_____

_____

The Master Within

It is through the intentional reflection of our experiences that we are able to capture the insight which lies within those moments. Reflect on what you have just experienced in this chapter, find the insight that lives within it, and take this moment to press those insights to paper.

_____

_____

_____

_____

_____

_____

_____

_____

_____

_____

_____

_____

_____

_____

Sports: Teamwork

EXECUTION

Execution, implementation, accomplishment, or whatever you prefer to call it… is the key to the creation of your masterpiece. When you execute with excellence, you position yourself for greatness. When you analyze actions, and make adjustments to find yourself in the winner's circle, you do so with the utilization of data collected from consistently executing at a high level. Creating a plan, plotting your course, and seeing yourself in your position, are all necessary steps to being where you want to be. None of them work unless you do. Your ability to execute will determine your ability to succeed. Vision without action, planning without execution, well, that's simply called dreaming. Now is the time for you to decide… are you a dreamer or a doer?

Taking action does not, and will not always mean doing the thing you thought "what if I could" about. Taking action does mean, however, always moving forward, and deciding to take and commit to a stance on a topic. A single brushstroke may determine the completion or start of a masterpiece, but it is the culmination of many colors, strokes, bristle sizes, and layers that make up the finished piece. The person who lacks action and demonstrates hesitation is likely to cause and experience great pain. Life has a way of reminding us just how important timing is. If we decide to delay our action or move too fast, it could result in us to having truly wasted the effort invested.

It should not be in question that we make time for the things in which we find value. Honestly, we make time for everything. We have far more control over our schedule, and the things that fill it than we may consider or even admit. The question should be, why do we not know this, or why do we not acknowledge it? We have the power to dictate our values, and standards, so we must have the power to have control over what we place first or second in our day. There are many situations in which we find ourselves feeling like we don't have options. As though we are stuck and without the ability to move or shift. The real truth is that we may have put ourselves in that very place in which we feel stuck. We may have made, or had a lot to do with, the life choices to take that job, have that child, get married, split up, take that promotion, go out on the town, or any other actions that lead to the place we currently find ourselves. Even in the very rare circumstances where someone else's will to act dictated our situation, we still have the ability and power to move, to shift, to control our outcome.

We can still control our day, our week, even our moment. This real truth is unshakable, and it is forever. You have the ability to take charge of your moment and dictate what comes next, and then what comes after that! Every action comes after thought. Every thought can be well thought out. We do not have to move from thought to action so quickly. Since we have power over time, then you have the ability to take time. You can take your time and dissect the layers of your thoughts. You then have the ability to refine those layers, and ensure that the presentation of those thoughts best represent your vision, and the desired outcome that you have for your actions.

If you consider each action as a piece to that magnificent mosaic, then would you best prepare them to stand long, stand strong, and come together to expose a brilliant work? Before your actions can be ready for success they must go through conditioning. They must be best prepared to weather the elements. They must know their place, and be willing to stand in that place even when they can not see the fullness of the completed work. Execution at such a high level, enhances self-awareness, improves situational leadership, and grows intestinal fortitude.

Taking a step back in a moment that one may desire to be reactive, so that person can implement such control, begins with a simple diagnosis of the circumstance. What are you trying to get out of your moment? What action will best get you there? Have you thought through the action? What outcomes may arise? What is the plan if your actions start creating an outcome other than what you were hoping for, planning for, and counting on? What if the action brings forth an outcome contradictory to the vision that you had? Did you really give your vision thought? Enough thought?

Remember that you have the ability to dictate your time and the ability to figure out what comes first, second, and third. You don't have to rush your actions. Just understand that if they show up too late, then they are wasted and become useless. This understanding is a key component to being prepared to organize your day. Just because you have the power to do this, doesn't mean you will get it right. You have been planning out your day and the actions you take each day and the question is "has that got you where you want to be?" Do you feel like you accomplish everything you hope to each day, or week? Are you winning in life and business on the level of getting the most out of your day? Do you take a moment and make it yours? Does a moment take your breath away more so than you breathe life into it? If a moment consumes you, can you see it happening? Are you able to reflect and adjust your course? Do you execute with excellence?

Asking questions, and looking for areas that require attention, or problem solving, is absolutely a form of taking action. So very many people only see the physical acts associated with solving a problem as ACTION. This is unfortunate, because, in reality, the seeking and searching for the answers to the problems that attack success are truly important actions. In fact, the importance of these actions often goes unnoticed to those not acting on them. Knowing the time is important, there is no doubt about that. Understanding who made the clock and how, are equally important things. Trusting the time displayed on the watch is easy to do, until another clock shows that its time and yours do not align. Do you disregard the time on the watch you own, or the one you just discovered? Why? Having the data is imperative if you are going to confidently decide whether your best move is to stay on, or correct your course.

Your perception is your reality, and for this reason you must allow part of the action you take to be mental action. What are you doing each day to set yourself up for the success you are seeking? Do you get down on yourself when you spend the day thinking through your plan but never get around to the physical action of executing? It is so vital to understand that I am not telling you to always be getting ready to get ready. It is more than that. I am saying that it is exponentially impactful to the outcome of your masterpiece for you to allow the due credit for the mental action you have been, and should be taking. There is a fine line between procrastination and being too aggressive in your action of doing. This boils down to the art of timing. Knowing when to let the idea continue to brew, to let it go, or to move forward with the vision of the strategy.

Remember at the beginning of this book, we discussed starting with the end in mind. A part of that process should be to give yourself goals with time limits. These can be adjusted, only when necessary, but should be in place at the beginning. If you find that you are constantly adjusting the timeframes set, then more evaluation should occur. When you give yourself life goals, meaning both personal and professional, it is essential to also set timeframes. These timeframes serve a purpose, and will refer you to either continue to move forward, shelf, or scrap the idea. There will be times when you want to hold onto something, and you may decide to place it on the shelf rather than scrap it. Be cautious with this. The shelf is for ideas that are worth further thought, energy, passion, and other resources. While you may have a surplus of one or more of these things, grasping the concept that time, energy, and resources are in limited supply, and should be used in places that will provide the most return, may aid in determining what stays, what goes, and what is valuable enough to come take space on your mental shelves and get put in line to be a future commitment for those resources. Understand that your capacity may very well be large, and, in fact, I tend to believe that it is larger than most realize, but if you do not respect your time and gifts, they will not respect you.

Continuing to actively invest bandwidth and resources on thoughts and projects, in general, must require your approval, your understanding of why that investment should continue to take place, and be worth it, at its core; even without your approval. When you start to take a mental position to the things you do, and have a true mindset of action you will find that it can be like a computer or smart phone. Even when you're not using a program it very well could be running in the background, and therefore taking up valuable space, speed, and other resources. When you start to understand that starting with the end in mind is something you can do in a moment, you will be able to further understand why having other programs, or unfinished thoughts and decisions running in the background is not only inefficient, but it can cause damage to your system.

I am not the authority on all things pertaining to execution. For, I have simply practiced being a sponge and soaking up as much information and as many beneficial moments that I have been able to get my hands on and wrap my head around. As a result, there is nothing more here than the life lessons I have learned, partnered with a lot of powerful information I have been able to inherit by understanding my place in life; and surrounding myself by individuals that know more, want more, and expect more than I do. Finding those people is hard, because I always strive to know more, have more, and be more. I am rarely

EXECUTION

unhappy with the place in which I am standing, or with the things I have. This is why I know that if I go further, get more, and always expect more, then I will find happiness there too. That is a large part of the HOW... How do I activate, and dial into a mindset that allows me to squeeze more juice out of the lemon at hand? How can I be more efficient with my time, thoughts, and results? It starts with understanding you must have an idea of where you are going so you can know where to begin and what getting there looks like. You must do more than know you want to go north... If you face south and start walking then you may get where you're going, but how long will that take you? Do you have the resources to weather that journey? You must only be working on the thought projects that should be running in the background. Do not overload your system. Writing down ideas, thoughts, and vision is a great way to get it out of your front of mind, but this doesn't generally remove it from the system. You must narrow your search so to speak. Think about what is important. What is it you really need to be committing to thought? Why do you need to be juggling all of those things at one time or at all? Remember, it is not only that we are able to take on a lot, but we are able to dig down to the core of things and mentally take action at a far deeper level.

This doesn't mean we should always do so. System overload is always just around the corner when we do this. After we understand that we must start with the end in mind, and then place ourselves on path that leads there, we must decide if that path gets us there in the fastest, most efficient and successful way. The 'most successful way' part of the prioritization equation could cause some issue for many.

You may be thinking that success is subjective and therefor this could be cause for too wide of a grey area. To that I say, no… Success is success, and if you think that what you consider successful differs from what someone else considers successful, and that is acceptable, I would like to adjust your thinking, should you be so open as to allow me. Consider this, two separate business owners have the same type of restaurant. They each opened the restaurant in the same market, in the same month, and with the same type of space. Three years later, one restaurant owner has opened two more restaurants while the other makes just enough to stay in business. Both owners consider themselves successful. Could this be a case of simply stating that one owner is right, and the other is wrong? Unfortunately, in many cases, both can be wrong.

Success is not up for discussion or debate. You can not simply will a bad decision into success. You can not assume you would get a grade of a "D" and when you make a "C" then say," well that is a success". It doesn't actually work that way with success, when you are looking at it correctly. Success is the results of walking in the right direction, at the right time, with the right tools, and achieving the goal you set out for when beginning the journey. When you are trying to find success, it requires great focus and attention to detail. Here is a way you can gain the focus you need to walk in the direction of the clarity needed to reach the place where focus lives. You must be able to shut down the works and projects that take up the needed bandwidth to overcome, and destroy the walls in the way of your next step and prevent them from blocking the path to the outcome that best serves the overall situation. This breathes life into a prioritization calculation that equals a winning recipe. Focus on your masterpiece.

A truth that people can often forget or misplace, is that deciding to do nothing, is still action. Deciding to do the wrong thing, or shelf something not worthy of shelving, are also actions. Admittedly, they are not productive actions, they are still actions. You can exert energy and act silly or you can act with intention and tear down the walls built between you and success. The mentality of action is not that you will cross the finish line, but that when you cross it, you will be the winner in a race between you and many others. A mentality of executing with excellence is one that understands the angle and best position for action, while never losing sight of the concept that the wrong action simply creates delays in the overall arrival of ones intended destination. Some actions can go as far as to take you off of and away from the path completely.

You see, you must get to the place mentally where your brain never sees a failure or stop, but rather a rerouting and updating of the anticipated arrival time. Your mentality must be "I will get there". I know where I am going, and I will get there. This must be a mentality that is so engrained in you, that it constantly reminds you from start to finish. This decision to execute with excellence has one's inner self stand up and decide that I will not only act, but I will do so with efficiency, care, attention to detail, focus, and diligence. You must be of the mindset that when an obstacle arises, you tell yourself "I will use one of the other resources, tools, and paths I have at the ready, because I have prepared for this moment". You must define your moments, have them be a real part of your success plan, and never let them steal from you the

EXECUTION

joy of victory. In your moment, you will be able to act with clarity, overcome changes in the course, tear down the walls of obstacles, and move in a way that brings forth the vision you set out with from the start.

You have placed yourself in the right starting point, facing the right direction for success. You have put together a plan and you made sure that this idea was worth the time to mentally act out the plan. You are moving at the right speed and with the right mindsets at the wheel. With this mentality of appropriate action, how could you be stopped, why would you slow down, what is able to defeat you. If your motives, and the spirit of your vision is one that is not serving others as well as yourself and if you have not involved the largest resource of a loving and caring God then perhaps you could be stopped, and your process be unable to do its job, but now you understand the last part of this way of life or mentality of action. You must include something far greater than yourself. You should always bring in not only the people in your life that know more, want more, and expect more; but that of Almighty God. For this simply brings your mental ability to the level required to have the discipline necessary to consistently execute with excellence. Consistently executing with excellence far surpasses the simple act of executing in a moment, it creates great action within. Great action, is action with all of these steps, and desires built into it. Great action is the difference between making art and creating your masterpiece.

I can hardly wait to see what masterpieces you will create.

It is through the intentional reflection of our experiences that we are able to capture the insight which lies within those moments. Reflect on what you have just experienced in this chapter, find the insight that lives within it, and take this moment to press those insights to paper.

THANK YOU

I've spent my life praying, thinking, speaking, wondering, hoping, and learning in preparation for this book. My life and the many experiences, places, and people within it have all played a significant role to help mold my ability to conceive the thoughts, direction, and way of believing that are necessary to breathe life into the concept of this book. The words, stories, and situations that I have placed in order to bring a reader to a starting point, and then walk them through a journey to reach the end with clarity and hope is not a short order, and something that I have been blessed to do, rather than simply something I have accomplished. Nothing of great value has ever been done all alone, and with no support. I am overwhelmed by the incredible insight, wisdom, and direction that many have poured into me, and as a result, this work of art, called "The Master Within." The truth is almost everything "Takes A Village" and this book was no different.

I want to take a moment to express my gratitude to the many heavy-lifters in the way of vendors, partners, and other key individuals who helped to check the boxes it takes to create a book, and see it to publication. From the editing, formatting, printing, graphics, suggestions, and so on. The collective efforts of those involved, have been such wonderful acts of true collaboration and synergy to bring this book to you, the reader. Thank you to each and every person who shared their eyes, voice, and hands in order to help make this happen.

I want to give glory and honor to my God. For the loving kindness of His grace and mercy. He saw fit to place inside of me the vision for this work, and the strength to bring it to life. I am so thankful to my Lord and Savior for all the blessings that have fallen upon my life. I acknowledge that without pain and sorrow, the joy of what comes in the morning is never fully appreciated. I know that even when times felt lonely and dark, the light of my life who is Christ Jesus was never far away. For this I am so thoughtfully and humbly thankful.

I want to thank my mother, Maryellen. She has always been a rock of hope and strength. The love, sacrifice and sense of resilience found inside her effort

Thank You

were inspiring as a child. The ability to always make me feel special and know that I have her trust, and loyalty was something every child should be able to hold on to. The truth is, I would be less of a man today if it were not for the work of my mother. Her friendship has never wavered. Her heart to be a person of value to everyone around her has always inspired me, and she is responsible for so many of the decisions I have made in my life to become who I am. I Thank you. I am grateful for you, far more than you could ever know Mom…

Thank you

The greatest level of thanks, recognition, and appreciation I would like to extend, aside from my God, is to my wife, and writing partner Christina Bartolotta. This book simply would not be a reality if it were not for the dedication, passion and effort of this strong and brilliant woman. The vision for this book and its concept was shaped by our hands, not just my own. The Word of Almighty God says that when you find a wife, you find a good thing. My wife has been my partner is every area of my life for over a decade at the time of this books release. It has been a labor of love to bring to her the thoughts in my mind, the emotions of my heart, and the words swimming inside my soul like strains of thread hoping to weave together a complete work. If it were not for her skill and talent to take all of that, and pour into it the very essence required to take the shape you see and read today, this book would be far less than what it has been called to be. The impact of its ability to bring greater hope, success, and breakthrough for its readers would never be so special, and for that I am so grateful for the words, thoughts, and dream my writing, and life partner Christina brought. My life and this work will forever be in her gracious debt. Thank you for always making me a better human. For watering my ability to stand tall, and lead. You are the very definition of a "Help Mate" and without your help I would fall short of the desire of my heart to be the kind of man, husband, father, and leader that is possible. You are my 100, and lack nothing I need to be complete.